SPIRITUAL WARFARE
Conquering the false j.u.d.a.h

Jezebel, Uzza, Delilah, Athaliah, and Hymanaeus are linked. All are bound and cast out by the Blood of Jesus. We exchange them for JESUS CHRIST and his good gifts.

BY SANDRA SUE BROWN

Spiritual Warfare- Conquering the false j.u.d.a.h

Written in 11-2011; revised 4-2012, 10-2013, 7-2015
Open Door- A Publishing and Training Center
PO Box 6511 in Hendersonville, NC 28793
jkeepprayingmom@yahoo.com
Copyright © 2015 Sandy Brown

ISBN-13: 9780692542361

Resources
Various Bible sources

King James Version- Public Domain

Wikipedia.com

Bible Dictionary
William Smith LLD, F.N. & M.A. Peloubet in 1884
The John C. Winston Co, Porter and Coates

DEDICATION

To
My Heavenly Father-God,
His Son, Jesus and the Holy Spirit.
To God be the glory, great things He has done.

ACKNOWLEGEMENTS

With love to my husband, Bill and my daughter, Penny and my whole family who prayed and encouraged me to get this information out to the Warriors and for me to get this book published.

This book, **Spiritual Warfare-Conquering the False j.u.d.a.h.**, is one of many in the **Just Keep Praying, Mom** series.

jkeepprayingmom@yahoo.com

CONTENTS

AUTHOR'S NOTE

Be wise and aware!

READ OUT LOUD all of the _underlined italics prayers_ that *appear while you are reading* this booklet! This is for you to be protected and cleansed from any influence of the evil ones being exposed by this booklet.

Section 1 - Check Your Mirror: Personal Prayer is First - urges you to repent of the evil in yourself that you see in others (Mirrors).

Section 2 - Study God's Word: Biblical Characters – References the Old and New Testament to give you the Biblical history about some of the people and their sins. I urge you to pray for freedom from the evil attitudes attached to the names.

Section 3 - Prayers for the Conquering Warrior - will encourage you to pray for yourself as you pray for others. as a spiritual Warrior. You are more than a conqueror.

SECTION 1
CHECK THE MIRROR
Personal Prayer is First

There are two types of mirrors: one is glass and the other is the people around you.

MIRROR 1: The first mirror includes your Prayers for Salvation, the Armor of God, and simple prayer guidelines

MIRROR 2: The second type of mirror comes from people who are around you, mostly the irritating ones, and simply praying for you to be set free from the same demons or attitudes.

SALVATION

Once one is saved by Jesus Christ, then He starts the cleansing process. Pray this prayer to get started on the life of a Christian.

Dear Lord God, I repent of my sins and I thank you for Jesus, who took them and gave me eternal life. Thank you for taking my sins of ignorance, and all the other sins I am not aware of. By faith, I know that I am saved from perishing. Amen

I ask for Your help, Holy Spirit, please fill me up with good gifts, including the Armor of God. Amen

ARMOR OF GOD

I put on the whole armor of God, gird up my loins with truth, putting on the breastplate of righteousness, shod my feet with the gospel of peace, put on the helmet of salvation, lift up the shield of faith and take the sword of the Word, then stand and pray for others... as described in Ephesians 6:10-19

PRAYER GUIDELINES

I claim a high tower, a hiding place and a hedge of protection for myself and my loved ones. While I am silent, I will listen for the Lord's hints or for a story from the Bible to use as my guide in all situations.

I claim a scripture... [ask for one! or use mine - 2 Timothy 1:7]:
"For God has not given me a spirit of fear, but of power, love and a sound mind." Amen

I will always pray in Jesus' Name,

LISTEN! FOR GOD TO SPEAK

Lord Jesus, I ask for God's discernment. Amen

Sometimes I "hear" a word or remember a scripture or a story that will help me with a specific problem.

FOCUS ON THE GOOD/ POSITIVES IN YOUR LIFE AND PRAY

I will limit my focus to the pleasant and positives of God. Lord Jesus, if I am lacking in knowledge, I ask for your help. Please give me a Mirror so I can repent of MY shortcomings. I will concentrate on the good and uplifting truths!

I know that there is freedom in concentrating on the gifts of God rather than on my efforts or on any ungodly thing. I love the blessings of God, but I will not ignore the negatives in my life such as the workings of the [devil/ satan] evil. Amen

Search me, O God and know my heart: test me and know my anxious thoughts: see if there is any wicked [offensive] way in me, and lead me in the way everlasting. Psalm 139:23-24

CHECK THE MIRROR

How does God show me? God gives me mirrors to see my anxious thoughts and offensive ways by using *IRRITATING* PEOPLE.

God gives me a mirror to help me see my own sins that I need to repent. This mirror is created by God to help me see my own problems, issues or demons. the mirror works by showing the disturbing actions or reactions in the people who are around me. God has shown me what I am doing so that (like in a mirror) I can see what needs to be cleaned up, but this time *spiritually cleaned.*

GOD USES DISOBEDIENT CHILDREN

God uses disobedient people or children as mirrors so that I can repent of my sin. The Lord God uses me to pray for churches that have demons, but first I repent of these problems in myself.

PRAYERS Not ANSWERED Immediately?

If I pray for others without dealing with my own needs first, my prayers are not effective. Matthew 6:12, "Forgive us our debts, as we have forgiven our debtors."

WHAT YOU SEE IN OTHERS IS
YOUR MIRROR FROM GOD

Sometimes my loving actions/words are misjudged as weird and rude. As a result, I am diminished in every way.
   My words are not impressive.
   My prayers are not effective.
   My walk is not matching my talk.
   My prayers are "sort of" unnecessary.
However, when I confess the sins that I see when I evaluate another person's actions and ask for God to cleanse me first of their sin, I am set free!
Once I do that, I can bind and cast out any demons that are connected to those sins in others, and I get God's blessing: Miracles happen!

I see more prayers answered when I confess any sins I see, I ask God to bind and cast out any demons and I pray for the blood of Jesus Christ to protect me. When I do this, Holy Spirit fills me up with His Presence and His blessings!

3

WITH GOD'S PRESENCE I am able to pray for others to be healed, delivered, and be changed. YES! I become a Conquering Warrior. I am blessed and they are blessed! Praise God! By submitting myself to a personal deliverance, my prayers are warmly welcomed and effective.
So repent now and let God show you why.

"If you see it, you be it ..."
It is your responsibility TO REPENT.

At first, I didn't see any need to ask for myself to be delivered from any demons. However, after studying, I realized that God wanted **me** to be delivered **first.**

God showed me I needed to get rid of the same things
that I saw in others!

I didn't want to admit it but God showed me that I had the same traits that I was seeing in others [my mirrors! Now I thank them.] When I meet people I don't like, I repent of having the same problem that they had, even if I didn't think I had their problem. If I confessed it anyway the Lord shows me how I was committing the same sin or when I was doing the same irritating thing!

Often, God would show me where I did the same **after** I repented! Having repented, I was able to pray effectively for the others to be healed and/or delivered. "Do not withhold good from those who deserve it, when it is in your power to act." Proverbs 3:27

The same is true if I am praying for a rebellious official, or a damaging or hurting church, or even a terrorist-filled country!

But there are times that you should not share with others. In Matthew 7:6 Jesus says, "Do not give to dogs what is sacred; do not throw your pearls before pigs. If you do, they may trample them under their feet, and then turn and tear you to pieces."

Of course, you should pray for others, but there is a time that you should not. That is when you are not forgiven or cleansed by God's forgiveness because you have not asked for God's forgiveness or because you have not forgiven someone.

"Therefore, if you are offering your gift at the altar and there remember that your brother or sister has something against you, leave your gift there in front of the altar. First go and be reconciled to them; then come and offer your gift." Matthew 5:23-24

In the Old Testament, the Levitical priest repented first of his sins, by coming before God with his offerings. Then he would offer a guilt offering and sin offering for the people.

Many sins may be hard to relate to but we should pray as King David was able to pray, "O God, search my heart and thoughts and show me the way." Ps 139:23-24

PRAY QUICKLY WHEN YOU ARE AWARE OF A PROBLEM

"In your anger do not sin: <u>do not let the sun go down</u> while you are still angry, and do not give the devil a foothold. He who has been stealing must steal no longer, but must work, doing something useful with his own hands, that he may have something to share with those in need." Ephesians 4:26-28

Lord Jesus, thank you for Your mirror. Please clean me up! Lord Jesus, I repent of what I see in others. I repent of not recognizing my sins and for not destroying any idols in my life. Before I study, I bind Jezebel, Uzza, Delilah, Athaliah, Hymanaeus, and all their demonic entities and cohorts. I bind and cast out all of these devils from myself. Lord God, fill these empty places with Your mercies, Your blessings, and Your everlasting love for Jesus and Your creation. Amen

If I notice some infraction or irritation in others I simply think or say the above or a similar prayer of repentance. At first I did not see an immediate change in me or the others, however I believe that God answered my prayer, because as I continued to pray this way, I noticed that my prayers were also being answered *more quickly*! AND I was praying in faith, and in God's will! Therefore, I reasoned that my prayers were being answered quickly by God to encourage me to continue this type of praying. Yes, and because it was creating humility when I asked God to deliver me.

The results?
I was being given prayers that were in God's perfect will! PLUS, it is easier for me to repent of any wrong, and take authority over demons that might want to harass me.

5

When I started doing this I was sick, in a great deal of pain and taking 8 pain pills a day and very weak. Now I am without pain, drug-free, and am much healthier! I have more energy to do God's bidding because I put off my falsehood. The devil has no foothold according to Eph 4:26-27. Being free of pain is a blessing from God.

Pain Affects Us in Many Ways

Pain, even good pain, affects us. Sometimes change produces emotional or physical pain. Personally, I don't like pain. I try to avoid it, but I have friends who seem to love pain. They love it when their muscles hurt or are pressed really hard. They can handle it. Not me, Yipes!

For me, pain is similar to scraping my fingernails on the chalkboard or walking in squeaky shoes. Even the thought of pain makes my spine tingle and my nerves go on edge. I do not like pain, so I try to avoid spiritually and physically painful things! If you are in my camp, pray this way: **MAKE IT EASY, LORD.**

These scriptures and prayers helped me.
Isaiah 26:7; Psalms 27:11; Psalms 23:3; Proverbs 4:11

I use these scriptural truths and I pray before any big changes that are coming into my life. Moving to a new place, new procedures at work, a new member is being added, or a significant holiday is coming, or there are disturbing events in the news, simple fears, and worries would elicit a 'make it easy' prayer, such as Psalms 5:8 or mine:
Help Lord Jesus, I am coming to a difficult time. Please, lead me, O Lord, in your righteousness because of my enemies- make straight [easy] your way before me.

If you don't mind being in pain, you can still pray for the Lord Jesus to help you get through a problem. You might also pray to God to enable you to be a godly witness, or pray that the necessary changes will bring glory to God.

Personally, I pray for help from God in any seemingly difficult situation and I plead with the Lord using Psalms 34:17: *Lord Jesus, "The righteous cry out, and the Lord hears them; he delivers them from all their troubles." Please Lord, help! I know I have to change, but 'make it easy'. Amen"*

When I pray this way, I believe that God answers my prayer and I know things are going to be as easy for me as He can make them. He is a loving Father God and He makes it easy when I ask or even yell, "Help me!" God also promises to deliver us from evil and He gives us a way out! See Matthew 6:13; Psalm 3:7; Psalm 34: 7, 19 To God be all the glory. Amen

When praying for myself or for others, I pray for the changes "to be easy" and for God to help me through the situation quickly. Whenever I see spiritual warfare could happen or is happening, I always ask God to HELP me or make it easier. When I do, He will show me how to handle the problem and how to pray. But I might not know His easiest way, if I do not repent of the sins of my Mirrors first.

REPENT

After I repent and ask the Lord to forgive me, I am able to recognize the evil that needs to be cast out. Having repented [and casting out the entities], I am generally more effective in my own Christian walk. Plus, I am ready to work for the Kingdom of God in helping others be set free as a Conquering Warrior. The last section of my book encourages the spiritual warrior.

ALL PREPARATION STARTS WITH ASKING

Lord Jesus, come into my heart and life. Save me from all my sins. Amen

Ask and it shall be given unto you...Luke 11:9

Then ask, *"How should I pray against these ungodly powers in others?"*

God has given me the desire to help churches and others who need to be cleansed. He has given me a love for others to be set free. Since I have been delivered, I am now ready to fight for others.

If the Lord directs me to learn about a particular negative, I know that He is going to give me a battle where I will need this gleaned information. Much preparation was required to write this booklet. Be ready for a battle unless you pray the prayers that have italics and are underlined.

Lord God, through the Holy Spirit, give me the power or authority and help me to recognize the demons that are to be cast out. First, God prepare me and then prepare me to help others. I believe that when I am prepared (hopefully through this booklet) that I will be ready for the time and season to war the False j.u.d.a.h. or any similar evil. Help me to become a warrior in Your army. Amen

7

GOD'S GOODNESS

I am in awe of Jesus Christ who takes our sins, demons, problems, and He gives us useful treasures!

HOWEVER, with these treasures/giftings there is a responsibility attached:

WE MUST USE THEM!

Lord Jesus, give me discernment, wisdom, knowledge and understanding. Amen.

When God gives us help, it will probably come in these forms: the gift of discernment, wisdom, knowledge, and understanding. He may also use our wisdom, knowledge, understanding, physical senses, Bible stories, our experiences or your Mirrors to identify the demons to be cast out.

Discernment:
> The gift of Discernment helps us identify an evil spirit and when to act or react to it. 1 Corinthians 12:10

Wisdom:
> The gift of wisdom enhances prudent answers and when you should use a scripture or story that God wants for a particular problem. James 1:5-6 and Proverbs 4:5-8

Knowledge with understanding:
> God will show the condemned demons to you. You will remember a scripture, by prophetic word or action. Past experiences may help to address any future deliverance. God is creative and so are you as His Warrior. Proverbs 1:10 and Proverbs 3:20

Help me Lord to use all the gifts you have given me, for your Glory. Amen

The Lord gives us our five [or six] senses, and He gives us His Word, the Bible stories from the Old and New Testament, and He will use our personal experiences.

Physical Senses:
> The five senses include sight, hearing, taste, touch, and/or smell, plus we have a spiritual sense. Use these senses for God's glory. Like Jesus, the believer is gifted with these senses to recognize the darkness. Isaiah 42:16

BIBLE STORIES:

By reading the Bible or a specific story, the warrior can identify an evil spirit or demons to be cast out. Reading God's Word and the Old Testament stories especially, will help the warrior to realize how to repent and how they have missed the mark with God, and finally, how to pray.

It is important to read about the people who have been against God, and since demons will take on the name of these people of the past, I am sensitive to demons, but they are like dirt. YES, dirt.

We have a great deal of dirt in our lives, even in our air, and we must not be afraid of dirt, unless we have too much. That is when we clean. Right!

There are two times <u>2x more</u> angels than the demons.

Please realize that there are some demons that are not harmful to us, they do not stop our doing the work God has called us to do. Be careful of those people who are always looking for demons.

I WANT JESUS to be FIRST in my life and thoughts! He is the One who sets us free!

However, when I become aware of a demon trying to work against another believer or it is affecting me or the body of Christ, I want to get rid of it. Suddenly, I have become a warrior and you can be too!

SECTION 2
STUDY GOD'S WORD-
Biblical Characters

IN JESUS' NAME, I bind and cast out the false j.u.d.a.h. JEZEBEL, UZZA, DELILAH, ATHALIAH, HYMANAEUS and All of their attached demons! Thank you Lord God, for filling me with Your Goodness. Amen.

The people who were evil in the Bible stories can also be people with similar demons in modern-day times. These demons are not personal traits, they are demons. To get deliverance and to be used in helping another get delivered, recognize the demon in your life [after you accept Jesus as Lord and Savior] and then by taking authority over any of them in your life.
Call another believer to help you, if you can.

Through God alone we are righteous and given authority to claim freedom for ourselves and for others who are in slavery to these demons. Isaiah 42:6-7 and 61:1 and Luke 4:18-19

LOOK IN YOUR MIRROR!

START by asking "*Jesus please come cleanse my life from sin. I ask for Holy Spirit to help me!*
Look in your mirror first!
I Repent of YOUR sinful characteristics and those listed.

11

<u>I Bind and cast them out in Jesus' Name</u>. List the evil things and give them to Jesus. Order each evil thing to leave.
<u>I Exchange</u> the evil and sinful for all of God's good gifts. Ephesians 4:22-24
<u>I Trust</u> that Jesus has already set you free by His dying on the cross and by being raised from the dead. John 8:36
<u>I Thank God</u> for His mercies being new every morning (as often as needed). Lam.3:23

*Pray the Lord's prayer- Matthew 6:9-13
Seal all the <u>good work</u>, and
Pray for <u>"no backlash"</u> Amen

Taking authority over demons does not require knowing where the demons came from but there is some information about the Biblical history for the names of these demons I have labeled or simply labeled as the "false j.u.d.a.h."

READ OUT LOUD **the underlined italic prayers** that appear while you are reading this booklet! Pray and learn about the Biblical history of these demons and others that are attached.

READ OUT LOUD the prayers that are included.
<u>As I read about these, I bind these demons from me and my loved ones. I repent of all the sins that are listed here! I claim Jesus' blood to cover me and my loved ones as I continue these steps of deliverance from the demons. Thank you Lord Jesus. Amen</u>

OMRI AND AHAB

Omri and Ahab were in Biblical times. King Omri worshipped the god Uzzi. Omri's son was Ahab who became the king of Israel. King Ahab was evil and married an evil woman. Both King Ahab and King Zedekiah were so evil that a curse was said over them by God's prophet, Jeremiah. There are demons that have the same names and/or characteristics and are called Ahab and Zedekiah.

Omri- was King of Israel and he was the father of Ahab. 1 Kings 16:25-26
Omri did evil more than all those before him, he committed **sins and worshipped worthless idols**, and walked in the **evil ways of Jeroboam**, he reigned 12 years and died   Ahab, son of Omri became King of Israel; I Kings 16:22-8 and 17:1
Ahab did more evil than Omri [and the others before him]:
rebelled against God

12

I bind Ahab and Zedekiah, and I repent of their sins and of worshipping worthless idols, and of their evil ways and of rebelling against God, in Jesus' Name. Amen
Ahab married Jezebel, a Baal priestess.
She started to kill all the prophets of God; **murder**
   they served and worshipped Baal: **idolatry,**
    built a temple to Baal and **set up an altar** in this Baal temple:
    blasphemy, evil, sexual sins, slavery
   made an **asherah pole** and did more to provoke the Lord: used
witchcraft, satanic worship, prostitution, human sacrifices

To quote Jeremiah 29:22, we find that Ahab and Zedekiah's names would be spoken as a curse.
  '"The Lord treat you like Zedekiah and Ahab, whom the king of Babylon burned in the fire." [Fire is likened to Hell, or damnation]
  "For they have done outrageous things in Israel; they have committed adultery with their neighbors' wives and in My Name have spoken lies, which [the Lord] did not tell them to do."

I repent of the worship of any other gods and the sins mentioned above or implied. I will only worship the Lord God Almighty and Jesus Christ. Help me, Holy Spirit! I am praying in the Name and Blood of Jesus. Amen

Ahab died in battle, even though he was in a disguise. He left behind his 17 year old son Ahaziah and the Queen Mother Jezebel. He reigned in Israel for 2 years, but King Ahaziah worshipped like his mother, Baal-Zebub the god of Ekron instead of the God of Israel. They led the people to idol worship, **consulting mediums, caused others to sin, and provoked the Lord, the God of Israel to anger.**

The young King Ahaziah fell through the lattice of his upper room and died. **death** Ahaziah had no sons 2 Ki 1:1-2 **barrenness**

Ahaziah's mother was Athaliah (granddaughter of Omri) and may have been trained by Jezebel. **ungodly, faulty teaching**

Jehu's soldiers wounded Ahaziah who died at Meggido 2 Ki 9:27 **confusion**

Joram, son of Ahab became king of Israel when King Ahaziah died. Joram (like Jeroboam, his relative) was **evil.** Joram only got rid of the sacred stone in temple of Baal. **half-hearted love for the Lord God**

13

Joram is killed in battle. He was hit by an arrow through the heart and his body was thrown in the field of Naboth **retribution** 2 Kings 3:1-3; 9:24

King JEHU was a good king. He reigned as ruler for 28 yrs 2 Ki 10:18-34

King and Warrior Jehu was an instrument of God's deliverance. 2 Ki 10:17

JEHU killed Jezebel, destroyed **Ahab,** and many of his **evil family,** seventy [70] sons including Joram and Nadab **death.**

JEHU and the other prophets who feared God killed the evil prophets of Baal, burned the sacred stone, and yet even he did not turn away from **other sins** 2 Kings 10:28-31

Dear Jesus, I repent of all these evils, in Jesus' Name. Amen

Demonic beings can be named the same as the people who exhibit their evil actions, ie. Ahab, Jezebel, Ahaziah, Joram, Zedekiah.
I bind these demons and claim Jesus' blood and protection for me and my loved ones. Amen
King Ahab was heir to the throne, he was royalty. As children of God, we are heirs to the throne with Jesus; we are royalty!

Ahab the King and the demon, was **placid, sniffling, and impotent.** He was **not following God. He worshipped false gods** and **spoke lies in God's Name.**
I repent of these sins of Ahab, in Jesus' Name. Amen
We are labeling this demonic being, Ahab.
I bind this demon Ahab and cast him out, in Jesus' Name. Amen
By repenting of Ahab's **traits** we are asking Jesus to deliver us from evil.

Jezebel's husband, King Ahab was Athaliah's father. She is linked to this evil grouping. Jezebel, the wife of Ahab, and can also be labeled as a demon.
Jezebel **worshipped Baal, offered human sacrifices to a false god, taught her husband, children and countrymen to turn away from God of Israel, murdered her adversaries and godly prophets, paid false prophets, prostitutes, and paid witnesses to speak lies.**

As I read about them, I bind these demons, minions and cohorts by the blood of Jesus. I claim God's protection for me and my loved ones. Amen

14

JEZEBEL

JEZEBEL had many demonic traits and I bind all of them in Jesus' Name. Amen

Jezebel was a very outspoken evil woman and because her husband was the king in his own right, she blatantly manipulated and worked the system to her favor to get what she wanted.
I Kings 22 and 2 Kings 9 **manipulation**

Jezebel's husband King Ahab was **whining** when he didn't get his way [to buy a piece of land]. Jezebel asked for the king's authority and Jezebel used the king's authority as her own. She **ordered the deaths of a good man** [Naboth] **and of many godly prophets**.

Jezebel took the position of "the boss" by manipulation and by **working the system** in her favor to get what she wanted. She **paid witnesses to lie** and got the land the king desired by having Naboth, the landowner killed.

She ordered the death of the good prophets and hired false witnesses to **legally kill the godly** man, Naboth for a tiny piece of land [it was his birthright!] and gave it to the **spoiled, sulking, pouting, resigning** King Ahab.
When Jezebel married the king, she **introduced her false gods and evil priests** to the people and to her children. She spoke **out loud demands and threats**, especially against God's prophet Elijah.

She **worshipped the idols of Baal** and she **paid for many false prophets** to come into Israel. Jezebel **hated and killed God's prophets,** more than 400 of the Lord's prophets. She was known for **destroying all of her enemies** swiftly.

When Elijah saw the idols and false gods being worshipped, he spoke out against her by predicting her death, but she spewed out a **pronouncement of death** on Elijah. Elijah fled to a cave.

I repent of all of Jezebel's evil including witchcraft, anger, and rage, in Jesus' Name.

Meanwhile King Ahab went to war and died in battle. To maintain **control,** Jezebel killed most of the royal persons who could assume the throne and she ruled for several years until she was killed upon JEHU's request. He and her two eunuchs threw her out of the window into the street and horses trampled her. Only her skull, feet and hands were found since the dogs ate her flesh.

15

ELIJAH, God's prophet, prophesied THE TRUTH!
Elijah said that there would be no dew or rain for 3 years. There wasn't.
Elijah prophesied the death of and slaughtered the prophets of Baal.
They were executed.
Elijah told how Jezebel would die and she was!
Elijah's prophetic word about Jezebel was fulfilled when the dogs ate the
flesh and left only her skull, feet and hands for burial. 2 Kings 9:35-37

JEZEBEL worshipped an evil god; she threatened and killed many godly
priests, and led people into sin. She performed human sacrifices, witchcraft and
used murder to get her way!

Jezebel vowed to kill Elijah. He worshipped our Living God and her curse
against him did not come to pass. Alleluia!!

*I repent of the sins mentioned and of any evil curses or actions. I repent of any worship of false
gods. I will worship only the Lord God Almighty and Jesus Christ.
Dear Holy Spirit, help me! I also agree that Jesus took the curse when he was crucified, rose
again and gave us everlasting Life in exchange. I pray in Jesus' Name. Amen*

*I claim freedom from all curses. A s I read about these, I bind these demons from me and my
loved ones, in Jesus' Name. Amen*

UZZA, HUBAL AND ALLAH

Al-Uzza [Uzza] was one of three goddesses. Hubal and Allah are linked to Uzza
and Baal. **idol worship, human trafficking, prostitution, lying**

In 2 Kings 21:18, 26 there is mentioned a Garden of Uzza, it was known as a
pleasure garden. Perhaps the two evil kings worshiped this goddess, Al-Uzza,
but the scriptures do not say but it does say that this garden was where King
Manasseh and his son, Amon were known to be buried. It was not a normal
place for kings and it is a known fact that they both did evil in the sight of the
Lord. That may have been the reason the people did not bury them with their
ancestors.

According to Wikipedia, Al-Uzza was one of the three chief goddesses of the
Arabian religion, pre-Islam. Uzza was the youngest and most powerful of the
three daughters of Allah. She was evil. Al-Uzza also appears in Ibn Ishaq's
account of the satanic Verses!

16

When they were in battle called Uhud, the war cry of the Qurayshites was "O people of Uzza, people of Hubal."

Uzza, Hubal are linked to Allah.

Hubal was a false god from pre-Islamic Arabia. Hubal possibly came from Syria or from the land of Hit in Mesopotamia, [modern day Syria and Iraq]. We know that Hubal was worshipped as a deity, over the Moon, Sun, Venus (evening star) and/or a warrior rain god. He may have also been called Baal. The Hubal idol was of a human figure, carved from red agate or "cornelian pearl", with its right hand broken off and replaced with a golden hand. **evil gain for wealth**

It was believed that by tossing seven "arrows in front of the statue" of Hubal and noting the "direction in which the arrows pointed answered the questions asked of the idol" regarding death, virginity, and marriage. **superstition**

I repent of superstition and desire for evil gain, in Jesus' Name. Amen

The image of Hubal was worshiped at the Kaaba mosque in Mecca., where there were some 360 other idols. Camels were offered as a sacrifice to these false gods. **animal sacrifices**
The article noted that 100 camels were sacrificed to save Muhammad's father's life when his grandfather asked which one of his 10 children should be offered to the god. **human sacrifices, generational curses**

Muhammad's father is reported to have brought the infant Muhammad himself before the image of Hubal. Hubal may be closely linked to Dushara and Manawatu [Manat], two other gods. **idolatry, abuse of all living things, abortion**

I repent of and break off the generational curses, abusive actions, and abortion. Amen

Later, Muhammad is quoted as asking Hubal for help, "Show your superiority Hubal."
Hubal was his father's god and he recognizes it when he went to battle.
But perhaps he did not win the battle.
Later, he asked Allah for help for the next battle, and Muhammad conquered Mecca in 630. It is reported that he removed and destroyed the statue of Hubal, along with 360 other images of gods, and re-dedicated the same structure to Allah. **idol worship**

17

Osama bin Laden has called 'America, the modern Hubal' and we know that Al Qaeda's number two man, Ayman al-Zawahiri, repeated the phrase ("hubal al-'asr") in describing America, during his November 2008 message and Barack Obama's election to the presidency. **cursing**

With God's help, we repent of idol worship and break all the curses and we immediately pray a blessing on America, through the blood of Jesus and in Jesus' Name.
I repent of the worship of any gods and of their sins mentioned or implied. I will worship the Lord God Almighty and Jesus Christ with the help of the Holy Spirit!

In Jesus' name, I also agree that Jesus took the curses when he was crucified, and that He arose again and gave us everlasting Life in exchange for death. Thank you for forgiving me and saving me, in Jesus' Name I pray. Amen

BLESSING UPON AMERICA

We ask for God's forgiveness and pray that the fire of God fill all of the empty places. We give God all the glory for doing this. Thank you Jesus. Amen.

We break this curse spoken over "America" and the United States of America, in Jesus' Name and ask that God's perfection and goodness fill the place. By the blood of Jesus, we claim freedom from any curses that Osama or his cohorts have spoken. Amen.

We agree that Uzza and her 2 sisters are bound with satan and we send them to the Cross of Jesus because Jesus is Lord over them! We declare that Hubal and the 360 gods, including Allah are removed and destroyed from America and from our United States of America's land and its leaders. Amen.

Pat Robertson in 2003 stated, "The struggle is whether Hubal, the Moon god of Mecca, known as Allah, is supreme, or whether the Judeo-Christian Jehovah God of the Bible is supreme," however, *We declare that the struggle is over and that the God of Abraham, Isaac and Jacob is Lord!*
Using my mirror teaching, if I see any evil in someone else, I will confess it as mine first and make sure I am cleansed of it before I pray for others.

Lord God I love you and worship You and You alone. Thank you Holy Spirit for cleansing me of all the sins mentioned or implied. I thank you for binding these demons mentioned by the same name and I place them at the foot of the cross of Jesus' blood.
Cleanse me of all sin and I bind and cast out all the demons. Thank you Jesus, I am Yours! and I pray for those people to be saved, cleansed, delivered, and totally committed to You, Lord Jesus. Amen   As I read about them, I bind these demons, minions and cohorts by the blood of Jesus. Amen

DELILAH & SAMSON
Judges 15, Joshua 15:33, Judges 13-16:4-18, Hebrews 11:32

As I read about the sins mentioned, I bind the connected demons, minions and cohorts, by the blood of Jesus. Amen

In Judges 15 and 16 we find the story of Samson and Delilah. Delilah is important because she was used **to deceive** and then **brought a man of God down** to his death, spiritually and physically. But God had the last word.
I repent of bringing down godly men and women and of deception. I claim healing in Jesus' Name. Amen

DELILAH, a Philistine, worshiped the false god, Dagon. Dagon was a fish god, the national god of the Philistines. It had the face of a man and the tail of a fish. **idol worship, slavery, familiar spirits** "The fish-like form was a natural emblem of fruitfulness and as such was likely to be adopted by seafaring tribes in the representation of their gods." In Gaza and Ashdod there were temples to this fish-god. The temple in Ashdod was destroyed by Jonathan in the Maccabaean wars. Traces of the false god Dagon appear in the names of Caphar-dagon and Beth-dagon found in Judah and Asher according to Joshua 15:41; Joshua 19:27 and I Samuel 5:5 **false gods, idolatry, human sacrifices/abortion**

Delilah, her brothers, and her rulers went against Samson several times. Delilah was faithful to her evil brethren/the rulers of the Philistines (Judges 16:5) instead of to her believing spouse. **bad decisions, antichrist** Delilah is complicated because there are so many parts and the demon with the same name is like her. **double-mindedness, divisive, deceit, lying to a man of God, misuse of persuasion, jealousy, verbal abusive, nagging, treachery, false accusations**

Delilah accused Samson of not loving her. Her name means languishing. Delilah used her beauty to **weaken** Samson, who worshipped the Living God. She **manipulated and whined** to get her way and she turned against him and God. She **compromised, tried to please her family and her political rulers instead of God, was faithless, unloving and did not worship the Lord God**

I repent of the sins mentioned and I claim freedom from all evil, in Jesus' Name. Amen.
I repent of all of Delilah's and Samson's sins and of their demonic characteristics and I claim total cleansing by Jesus' blood.

19

I repent of all connections to Delilah and of Samson and any other gods mentioned or implied. I choose to worship the Lord God Almighty and Jesus Christ. Holy Spirit, help me! I repent of taking any of the glory from God. I also agree that Jesus took all these curses incurred on the cross when he was crucified. I rejoice that He rose again and gave us everlasting Life in exchange. Amen

SAMSON means 'to be like the sun'. Samson was recognized as a judge but was diminished by his own actions and by the **lust for women.** One of the women was a Philistine woman, a non-believer, her name was Delilah. Since he wasn't following God, Samson allowed a spiritual door to open for satan and evil. **not choosing God's best**

Samson **abused his God-given gifts.** Samson was an attractive man but full of pride. He was willing to go against his parent's rules for his personal gain. **rebellious** His uncut hair and extraordinary strength were signs of being dedicated to the God of Israel. Samson had been dedicated to God, but Samson carelessly married out of **lust.** This **dishonored his parents.** He went outside God's protection, even though God had given him extraordinary strength, he was **self-seeking and willful.** He thought no one would catch him. **devious, sarcasm** He did repent, but not until late in his life.

He **rebelled and married** the non-believer. Then Samson caved in to Delilah who **pleaded and badgered** him to tell her his secret, ie. where he got his strength. When Delilah cut off his hair, Samson's strength [from God]was gone. The priests of her community were able to capture him and put him in prison. **wasted life, bad example to others, slow to learn, foolish**

When Samson gave in to Delilah, he was caught! as a result, Samson was shorn, blinded, shackled, and humiliated by the enemy and by Delilah's idol worshipping relatives and rulers, the Philistines. **overtaken by the enemies of God**

Samson was humiliated by being captured and then they gouged out his eyes, making him blind. Because of the **pride of life, lust of the eyes, and lust of the flesh,** Samson **ignored God's best** and was **lured by the beauty of ungodly women.** But in prison, it is obvious that he repented of his ways. His hair grew and so did his strength.

Samson's strength returned when he repented. *I repent as well.*

Samson's hair grew, his desire for God returned, and he was able to fulfill God's purpose. In the end, blind but rededicated Samson destroyed more enemies than he had previously. God used Samson to destroy all of his captors by giving him the strength to pull down their palace roof. Samson gave God all the glory. Sadly, his life was taken as well. [He probably destroyed the statue of Dagon their god, and even Delilah, by pulling down the whole Philistine building at its pillars.] **idolatry**

Samson is remembered and counted as a good judge, because God got the glory in the end. Samson was a good person with good parents, but he went against God. **unearned righteous heritage, in the flesh, running own show, proud of the giftedness and good looks, pride, vanity**

I repent of all the sins that Samson committed and pray for a hedge of protection around myself and my loved ones, in Jesus' Name. Amen.
As I read about them, I bind these demons, minions and cohorts by the blood of Jesus. Amen

I repent of all the sins of Samson and Delilah committed and for worshipping any false gods mentioned or implied. I determine to always worship the Lord God Almighty and Jesus Christ. Holy Spirit, help me! Jesus took all of my sins on Himself and by His blood I am set free. I accept His sin-free Life in exchange, in Jesus' name. Amen

ATHALIAH, JEHORAM AND AHAZIAH

After the King Ahab was killed in battle, Jezebel killed all the godly priests that posed a threat to her **controlling** the kingdom. Athaliah was **evil**, like Jezebel and her son, Ahaziah.

Jezebel trained her son to **consult mediums** and when he died, and when Jezebel died, Athaliah did more evil and proceeded to **destroy the rest** of the royal family [except one year old, Joash].

Athaliah was Ahab's [and probably Jezebel's] daughter. I believe that she was raised by Jezebel, her mother and she did what her mother told her to do.

Athaliah's grandfather was King Omri, and her father was probably King Ahab, who were both **undecided about God** and **weak**. Both of them **did not used their authority for God's glory**. Athaliah was very gifted but **strong willed**. She followed her mother's example by using her gifts to **worship the false god, Baal**.
Jehoram and Athaliah married. He was the son of Jehoshaphat and Jehoram became King of Judah. They **did evil in the eyes of the Lord**. *Edom and Libnah* **continue to rebel** against Judah.] 2 Kings 8:16-26

21

Athaliah bore King Jehoram [Joram]'s son, Ahaziah. When the king was wounded and died, Ahaziah became King of Judah. Athaliah became Queen Mother. When Ahaziah died, she murdered all in line for the kingship, except one, to keep in **control. murder**

Athaliah was taught by Jezebel to do **evil and idolatry** and she did not depart from it. She continued the **worship of Baal.** She had legal rights as Queen, after her husband and son were killed but sadly, she **used her authority for evil. killing babies to appease a false god**

Lord Jesus, I repent of taking control, murdering, and idolatry; cleanse me in Jesus' blood. Amen

Having killed all of her competition for the throne, she became Queen of Judah for 3-6 years. The priest Jehoiada made a covenant with the soldiers to overthrow her and they did. 2 Kings 11:4, 15-16

Meanwhile Elisha anointed Jehu to be King of Israel. Ahaziah and Jezebel were killed by Jehu   According to the prophetic word of Elijah the Tishbite. 1 Kings 21:23; 2 Kings 9:1-13 and 9:22-37 Athaliah failed to kill Joash, son of Ahaziah, because the daughter of King Jehoram [Joram], sister of Ahaziah, [Aunt] Jehosheba took Joash, along with his nurse, and hid them in the temple of the Lord.

With the help of a godly priest, JEHOIADA, Joash was hidden for 6 years. 2 Kings 11:1-3 **deception, hiding the truth**

Joash- at age 7 started to reign as a good king of Israel. 2 Kings 11:21 and 2 Kings 12:4-20 Joash's mother, Zibiah (an Israelite from Beersheba) was probably the Queen Mother.

I repent of hiding the truth and deception and pray for healing in Jesus' Name. Amen
Athaliah was murdered as well as Mattan the priest of Baal per the orders of Jehoiada, the priest. **murder**
2 Kings 12:12; Kings 10:13; 2 Kings 11:16-18; 2 Kings 12
        Joash was a good king and reigned for 40 years.

As I read about them, I bind these demons, minions and cohorts by the blood of Jesus. Amen

MY THOUGHTS ABOUT ATHALIAH

We know that Ahab's father Omri was Athaliah's grandfather but there is no mention of her mother. 2 Kings 8:26, "But since Athaliah was evil, and her child was Ahaziah they were related to Ahab's family by marriage. Ahab did evil in the sight of the Lord." I believe he and Jezebel had a great deal of influence on Athaliah and Ahaziah, her grandson. The facts about the Biblical person Athaliah and the darkened words are typical to the demon called Athaliah.

Fight with faith, **repent of the negatives** with the following prayers that address the sins of Athaliah. Athaliah was probably trained by Jezebel.**did not follow the Lord God**

Athaliah was very submissive to authority for a season until she gained control. **conniving** In **control**, she murdered all the royal family that she could get her hands on. **murdered rightful heirs**

Athaliah ruled the country for 6 years and was finally killed with a sword at the palace. 2 Kings11:3; 11:20 Mattan, her priest of Baal was also killed by Jehoiada. 2 Kings 11:16-18 **idolatry**

She did not worship God and she worshipped and made sacrifices to idols. Her offspring was evil, and they are under her control. **followed a bad example, needed control, led others to sin**
Athaliah gained authority and committed murder to keep her control. **created fear in others**

I repent of all the mentioned sins and I repent of worshipping any false gods mentioned or implied. I wish to worship the Lord God Almighty, Jesus Christ and Holy Spirit and to worship Him alone. In Jesus' name, I claim freedom from being a bad example, from needing to be in control, from being a bully and leading others into sinning. Thank you Jesus. Amen

As I read about them, I bind these demons, minions and cohorts by the blood of Jesus. Amen

HYMANAEUS

Hymanaeus was instrumental in damaging or destroying the faith of the new Christians. According to the research, Hymanaeus created a spiritual **gangrene** in the body of Christ during the time of St. Paul, the Apostle.
1 Timothy 1:20 and 2 Timothy 2:17-18

This one man Hymanaeus was also an **evil influence** on others, including

23

Alexander, an Ephesian Christian and on a man named Philetus, who became a disciple of Hymanaeus. Apostle Paul turned him over to satan and treated them as heathen because Hymanaeus believed and taught that the doctrine of **resurrection was just a metaphor** and that Jesus arose in spirit only. This is a false doctrine and it lives today in a person who is demon-possessed.

These deceiving teachers proclaimed that the resurrection had already taken place and were leading people away from the Truth of eternal life. The false teachers were saying that there would not be a resurrection for them as well. *Forgive me as I repent of leading a believer away from Truth of Jesus being raised in body and spirit. Amen*

Obviously, the Apostle Paul [2 Tim:17] was angry at satan for allowing these men to tear down the Faith and for deceiving the believers into thinking that Jesus was not resurrected bodily. He cursed them. I believe that Paul delivered them to satan so that they could repent.

This **deceiver demon, Hymanaeus** has entered our churches today and is continuing this **false teaching** that Jesus did not resurrect in a real human body, by saying that Jesus did not raise from the dead in body and spirit and that He does not dwell in us believers! **denying miracles, healing, signs and wonders, and tongues**

PRAY! I repent of any false teaching and any deception I have spoken, thought, or taught under the influence of Hymanaeus. In Jesus' name, I also agree that Jesus was crucified but arose again as fully God and fully man, and that I will be resurrected into Everlasting Life. Amen

I repent of all the previously mentioned characteristics of any of these demons. I bind and cast out all of these demons and anything connected with them. By Jesus' blood, I pray. Thank you Jesus Christ of Nazareth! Thank you for setting me free and for filling the empty places with your Holy Spirit and with good gifts. Amen

SECTION 3
PRAYERS
FOR THE
CONQUERING WARRIOR

God gives the Warrior the authority to fight against these demons and He will give authority and insight to you because you are more than a conqueror through Christ. I believe the Lord God helps some people can get free without any human help, but most of us need help and agreement. We ought to go to people with the gift of faith for our personal deliverance. I call these people Warriors.

I have found that these demons can be bound and cast out as one entity called the False j.u.d.a.h.. Not to be confused with Judah, I put periods behind each letter. Each letter includes more than one demon, but it helps the Warrior to remember the major demons. The demons called Jezebel with Ahab and Athaliah can be bound together. Samson is linked with Delilah and all of their minions. Uzza is bound together with Baal, Allah, and Omri along with more than 360 other demons. Hymanaeus, Alexander and Philetus are names of false doctrine demons and can also be lumped together with all the other cohorts that remain in this nest of demons, that I call the False j.u.d.a.h. .

Since they all are evil and were against God and the good people in the Bible, they all must be bound by the Blood of Jesus and cast out in Jesus' Name. We continue by declaring that the work is sealed and that we have no backlash or retribution, [Amen.]

25

When people get saved but have been hurt by these demons, they know about these evils through their own personal life experiences. They are eager to help others get free from any evil entities. When they are freed from the evils ones, they know that God set them free! Jesus read Isaiah 61:1b about Himself!
He has sent me to bind up the brokenhearted, to proclaim freedom for the captives and release from darkness for the prisoners...

However, many wonderful Christian people do not ask for this gift of healing because they do not want the responsibility and they would rather leave the warriors to do those battles that may arise. They may ask for other giftings, but without the gift of discernment, they may entertain evil. Lord, help them. *Lord, Please give me your gift of discernment.*

GOD'S WARRIORS

GODLY WARRIORS fought against the evil ones throughout the Holy Bible. There were and are godly warriors in the Holy Spirit. These warriors were sent by God to bring justice. God will always assign warriors when there is a need, like Jehu,and Jehoiadah, and the Apostle Paul.

Using the Gospel of love, you can fight against many bad teachings by applying God's Word.

First, by repenting of listening to and teaching false doctrine and casting out any demons connected. Then by binding and casting out the religious demons from you. Finally, by binding them until they are cast out from your loved ones, church, nation. You need them to agree for lasting results.

I have found that Jezebel, Athaliah can be bound together with Delilah. Hymanaeus and Alexander and Philetus can also be lumped together with all their cohorts. Since they all were evil and were against the good people in the Bible, I hope you can recognize them and their assisting demons. Use your mirror and destroy them by God's Righteousness.

GOOD EXAMPLES OF WARRIORS
We could be like Jehu or those eunuchs who helped throw down an evil ruler, Jezebel (2 Kings 9:30-37)
We could be the Someone who helped Jehu (1 Kings 22:34)
We can anoint the next king (2 Kings 10:23-28).

26

We can repair the temple/church and/or we can bargain for peace (2 Kings 12)

We could be an unnamed little prophet to warn a king.

KNOWN OR UNKNOWN WARRIORS

A priest fought alongside some of the commanders of one hundred soldiers. Other nameless men were given David's spears and shields. They fought for the Lord.

A well-known prophet spoke the truth to an idol worshipper and also prophesied a warning of future demise.

We could be like the aunt or babysitter who would protect a little child from harm.

The Apostle Paul fought against **many bad teachings.** We have the same battles today.

In the Holy Spirit, we can be warriors by applying God's Word to a situation or apply a healing balm.

Lord Jesus, all of your warriors are important. I repent of not warring when I should. Forgive me and wash me clean to face another battle for Your Kingdom. Amen

HOW CAN WE BE WARRIORS?

How? We can with the anointing of God, Use Jehu, the Apostle Paul and unknown Warriors who fought for the Lord as your godly examples.

Beware of others such as King Joram of Israel and Ahaziah, king of Judah symbolized **idolatry, witchcraft and passivity.** Both were overthrown by Jehu. You can be a spiritual warrior like Jehu and take authority over these demons, taking authority over them for YOURSELF **FIRST**!

In Jesus' Name, I bind them* and cast out idolatry, witchcraft, and passivity of me. I repent of any worship of any gods, their sins mentioned or implied. I bind them and ask for God's anointing to cleanse my whole territory by the blood of Jesus. I wish to worship the Lord God Almighty. Lord God, fill me up with your good gifts, righteousness, trust, boldness and more blessings.

27

In Jesus' name, I also agree that Jesus took all the curses when he was crucified and rose again in body and spirit. I believe that God has given us Everlasting Life and many spiritual gifts [love, joy, peace, goodness, kindness, long suffering] in exchange for every sin. AMEN

* When deliverance is needed for yourself and others, all of the evil characteristics mentioned can be combined [as the False j.u.d.a.h.], bind them and cast them out, in the Name and Blood of Jesus.

PRAYERS THAT CAN START THE PROCESS OF DELIVERANCE FOR YOU.

Dear God, I come to You in the precious Name of Jesus, please forgive me for allowing evil in my life. I choose to receive God's forgiveness and to forgive myself.

I claim that no weapon formed against me or mine shall prosper. I confess the sin of my ancestors, my parents, especially my mothers, and my own sin of allowing Leviathan (the demon that produces misunderstanding, being misunderstood, and who flips words in normal conversation).

I renounce all vows and I break this curse from my life and from the lives of my descendants. Through the redemptive work of Christ on the Cross, I receive God's freedom from Leviathan, any vows I make and all generational curses. I pray that God replaces this evil with blessings of being understood and being able to understand. Amen Thank you Jesus for my cleansing and my healing. Amen

CLEANSING THE WARRIORS

BE A BELIEVER
Becoming a warrior: ALWAYS be sure the believer [warrior] is saved by the blood of Jesus Christ. Romans 10:3, 4-5, 9-11

REPENT OF "DIRT"
When "dirt" is identified during the battle, remember to repent of it yourself. I John 1:7-8

To avoid demonic activity, all of the warriors must know Jesus on a personal level and the warrior must recognize that there is the possibility of having to cast out personal demons but if he is willing to cast out any demon, there is no problem. Ephesians 4:25-31

For most people, a cleansing is needed on a basic level, but a deeper cleansing may be needed. It is similar to taking a bath on a regular basis and after a dirty job to have a needed scrubbing. When you identify the "spiritual or demonic dirt", please remember to cleanse yourself before going into a new spiritual battle. Remember to repent of the dirt first and then pray for yourself and then help others. Check your mirror first!

SHUT DOORS THAT LEAD TO ATTACK
The warrior must address the open doors that allowed evil to enter. Holy Spirit-led counseling or personal deliverance will help prepare the warrior. With God's help, the warrior will recognize the ways that the enemy can trick a believer and he will know how to pray for the doorways to be eliminated, such as, to stop drinking alcohol, drugs, lying, cheating, or gossiping. *I repent of these sins in Ephesians 4:25-31 in Jesus' name.*

ASK GOD TO PREPARE YOU
Jesus was prepared for the battle. In Matthew, He shows us how. Matthew 4:1-11 The Apostles were shown how to deal with demons by the Holy Spirit. Acts 8:20-24 and Acts 11:9 We can expect the same instructions during a hands on situation.

LISTEN FOR GOD'S VOICE. Acts 10:13-15
I have been shown what physical items need to be removed while praying for the person or place. This activity of listening may indicate which evil spirits need to be addressed/bound and cast out. I may discern a certain Bible character. There are demons that go by the same name as the stories found in the scriptures, either Old or New Testaments. That is why I have included the primary deliverance prayer at the beginning of this booklet.

DELIVERED AND HEALED
In my experience, repentance and physical deliverance/cleansing is generally done first by an act of will, then God heals any attached emotions. When one has stopped and separated themselves from a temptation, God can heal and enable them to help others with physical and emotional healing. Isaiah 42:7

I have seen people healed emotionally and delivered with no desire to sin again in that area. However, some have to continue in faith and claim they are free even though they are still struggling. To bind and cast out evil ones in the Name of Jesus is not enough to <u>stay</u> cleansed, you must also fill yourself with God's blessings. One must believe that God has done the total healing and He will continue [in His timing.] Ask and Believe. Luke 11:9-14

STEPS FOR LEADING OTHERS TO HEALING AND DELIVERANCE

First. Repent of sin, be baptized, and receive the Holy Ghost (Spirit)
Lord Jesus come into every part of my heart and life.
I demand that any demon be bound and I give it to Jesus and refuse/ or cast it out.
I ask for protection and thank you for the next step in setting my friend free.

SET FREE the person, minister, church, house, or territory in Jesus' Name and His blood. Acts 2:38-39; Matt 12:29; Matt 16:19
I bind this demon and, **with their agreement,** *it is cast out in Jesus' Name. Amen.*

Pray again: [sample of a prayer]
I repent of my sins.
I ask Jesus Christ to come into my life...all of the parts of my life [I claim my salvation]
I ask for God's help and Holy Spirit power [I claim the baptism] and I am washed by Jesus' blood. Heb 9:14
I rebuke and cast out any demons now! [I claim deliverance] Mark 3:15; 2 Tim 2:19

I will not entertain them again, if they try to return [I claim my sanctification]. *2 Tim 2:21*
Jesus, Please show me daily [I claim a gift of discernment or a good gift] if there is any area of my life that needs to be cleansed. Matt. 6:9-13

MORE PRAYERS

Thank you Jesus for helping me recognize Jezebel, Delilah, and Athaliah, Jezebel's husband Ahab, Athaliah's husband, Jehoram, and the brothers of Delilah, Ahaziah, Hazael, Matan, Baal, Asherah, and the Kingdom or House of Omri plus the other demons connected with them and Hymanaeus, Alexander, and Philetus. I recognize these anti-Christ spirits and they are bound in Jesus' Name.

All of the demons are bound and cast out of me. I give them to Jesus.
I give thanks to God for getting rid of all of them and for replacing them with the blessings of the Holy Spirit. Come Lord Jesus into these empty spots.

Therefore, I believe God has given me authority over these and I bind them and cast them away from those I love, and from this church and from this territory. I claim this place for

Jesus Christ and declare it is filled up with God's Holy Presence. To God, to the God of
Abraham, Isaac and Jacob. be all the glory.
I lift up my arms in thanksgiving and I give praise to the King of kings and Lord of Lords,
Jesus Christ. Who the Son sets free is free in deed. Thank you God, You are my beloved and
I am yours. Your banner over me is Love.

I am covered by the blood of Jesus Christ of Nazareth and I have the whole armor of God on,
according to Ephesians 6: 11-18.
I ask for a hedge of protection for me over my families, my property and around those I pray
for and for those who pray for me.

I repent of tall the sins found in Jezebel, Uzza, Delilah, Athaliah, and all their other demons
that are connected to them. I repent of any faulty teachings similar to the ones of Hymanaeus,
Alexander, and Philetus and others and pray for forgiveness.

I take authority over, bind and cast out all of these evil ones, in Jesus' Name. I give them to
Jesus Christ of Nazareth, My Savior and Healer. Now I ask that the Peace of Jerusalem fill
up all of these empty places. Amen.

There are more prayers to list the specific sins that can be said:

I confess idolatry, killing off the competition, going against and murdering the innocent,
belittling the anointed ones by my words and/ or my deeds, of conniving, of manipulation, and
all wickedness, witchcraft, deception, of being a people pleaser, of nagging, whining, wanting to
do it my way, of rage, and any others that I have missed but are linked.

I repent of going to any prophet or a false god instead of to the Living God for His healing
touch and for the Truth. I repent of deception, of trying to take control, of focusing on my own
agenda, and for not cutting off the strings of any familiar spirits I received. I repent of abuse
and misuse of the my loved ones, my talents and my gifts.

Remember to ask for and thank God for his forgiveness, His
righteousness and blessings:
Thank you God for Your forgiveness and I ask You to help me stay in Your will.

Fill me up Lord God with your Truth, Love, and the gift of the Holy Ghost.
I claim that the Holy Spirit will have His way in my life. I pray that the ones I am praying
for will know You as Lord. I claim freedom for them to be able to set others free.

Declarations are also in order after you are cleansed and refilled:
I declare that the enemy is defeated and all doors will be open to Jesus.
I claim that no weapon formed against me or those I pray for will prosper.

I claim that there is no backlash from the enemy.

I pray that the Holy Spirit will seal all of the good work done and ask that the way is prepared for more to come. I praise You O God for breaking all the curses, Amen

After I finished this study and prayed for my needs, I started to pray against the demons that ruled in these stories and against some of the mistakes that the Bible character had made. We have the same issues today, but there may be demons with the same characteristics as well. These need to be cast out through the Holy Spirit and exchanged or replaced with God's blessings.

2 Kings 6:16 has a great encouragement for those who believe in God, our Jesus Christ. "Don't be afraid,[Elijah] the prophet answered, **"Those who are with us are more than those who are with them."**

WE NEED EACH OTHER

After I bound and cast out these evils, I knew I needed to start praying for my family, friends, and others including my church, community, and then I started praying for our world to be free.
I pray that I will always be covered by the Blood of Jesus, and the armor of God and that God will help me in times of trouble and show me those people and places that you want me to pray for in Jesus' Name. Amen
Always be alert to any new lessons that God will teach you after this prayer.
With Jesus as My God, Lord and Savior, I desire to help others to be set free. Amen

JEHOIADAH

We must beware of doing good but stopping short of God's best. A warrior priest like Jehoiadah did several mighty deeds to stop evil but stopped short of righteousness.
The mighty deeds Jehoiadah did are many including:
He served God during Athaliah's reign.
Jehoiadah protected Baby Joash for 6 long years after Athaliah murdered all the royal family except for Joash.
He appointed officers over the house of the Lord.
He approved of the destruction of the Baal temple, prophets, and Baal priest, Mattan. He had the Baal temple torn down. 2 Kings 11:18
Jehoiadah helped his king to repair the temple of God. 2 King 12:9
He battled for the 7 yr old youngster king, Jehoash. 2 Kings 11:4, 21
Jehoiadah ordered Athaliah to be killed. 2 Kings 11:15-17

He made a covenant between the Lord and the king

Jehoiadah killed the Baal prophets after killing Mattan, the Baal priest. But, he did not destroy the golden calves of Dan and Bethel. 2 Kings 11:18 and 2 Kings 10:23-28 **not destroying all evil** Jehoiahah stopped short of destroying the golden calves.
Help me and forgive me for stopping short of your best and leaning on my own abilitiy rather than trusting you for victory. Amen

CLEANSING FOR THE WARRIOR
IS AN ON-GOING PROCESS

Keep in mind that we are human and will need "baths" once in awhile. Even though Jehoiadah was a victorious warrior and his name is mentioned as good, he was flawed and needed God to forgive and "cleanse" him. I recognize him for starting a good job, but he did not finish it. He did not destroy the golden calves. Those idols were the downfall to many of the other kings who followed.

The reader can read all of my prayers as the Lord leads and be cleansed; God is still working on us. We all still need correction, prayer, and to be made aware of our faults! Cleansing for the Warrior is an on-going process.

When a friend said he did not see humility in me, I asked him to pray for me to be free, right on the spot! Praise God for His Love and my friend's concern for me! We proclaim and declare that God is first in their lives and we say out loud "Jesus Christ is Lord". We know in our hearts that God raised Jesus from the dead in body and spirit. We know that Jesus is alive.

He is still working in our lives and I hope this book helps you along the way. May we continue to do His will and know that He will help us, in Jesus' Name and by His blood; we have the same hope and promises that are in the Old and New Testament. Amen.

BE BLESSED AND A BLESSING!